What Was It Like Marrying in the 80s?

A Journal (for Her) to Revisit and Share 80s Wedding Bliss

~ Riya Aarini ~

What Was It Like Marrying in the 80s?
A Journal (for Her) to Revisit and Share 80s Wedding Bliss
Text Copyright © 2025 by Riya Aarini

ISBN: 978-1-956496-66-6 (paperback)
ISBN: 978-1-956496-67-3 (hardcover)

www.riyapresents.com

This book belongs to '80s bride

_____

_____

Contents

Welcome to Your '80s Wedding!

A wedding is a once-in-a-lifetime celebration attended by beloved friends and family who travel from near and far to witness the special occasion. It is equally a subject of joyful reminiscence.

A traditional '80s wedding is truly recognizable. Wedding wardrobes offered theatrical flair, with billowy bridal gowns expressing the decade's opulence. The ceremony itself remains memorable to brides who created joyous atmospheres with lively '80s music, delicious (sometimes homecooked) food, and dancing. But what elevated '80s weddings was the genuine love couples felt for each other. These budding romances inspired excitement and happiness, marking the ceremonies as unforgettable.

Take a trip down memory lane via this journal and share what made your '80s wedding spectacular. Whether you spent $800 or $8,000, the spirit and glamour of your '80s wedding deserve to be shared!

First Acquaintance

How did you first meet your soon-to-be spouse?

Where did the introduction occur? Describe the sights, sounds, and scents.

What thoughts ran through your mind?

Describe whether it was "love at first sight" or "love a while later."

If your heart skipped a beat, did you instinctively know you'd marry this person?

Dating

If your heart didn't instantly flip on your first acquaintance, how far into dating did you realize this person would become your spouse?

How long did you date before becoming engaged?

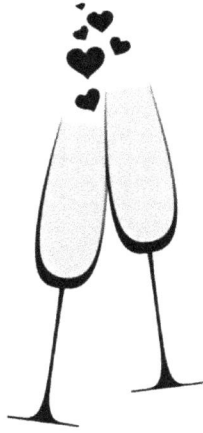

Engagement

Where did your significant other propose?

Did it come as a surprise?

How emotional was the moment? Did you feel relief, comfort, excitement, something else?

How long were you engaged?

Engagement Ring

Many '80s brides desired the timeless round-cut diamond solitaires, while others favored more daring styles of engagement rings.

Was your '80s engagement ring embellished with diamonds or gemstones?

If diamonds, in what shapes and cuts?

If gemstones, which ones?

Did you prefer the yellow-gold bands trending in the '80s?

Describe whether your engagement ring was simple or ornate.

How much did your engagement ring cost?

Was your engagement ring set with gemstones handed down from prior generations? If so, describe the stones and their significance.

Wedding Planning

Did you plan for a small, intimate wedding or an over-the-top production? What influenced your decision?

How far in advance did you start planning your '80s wedding?

How many days, weeks, or months did it take to plan your wedding?

List the key individuals involved in your wedding preparations.

Did you hire a wedding planner?

What was your wedding date?

Did you consider this date auspicious, or did it hold sentimental
value?

Invitations

The era's wedding invites consisted of vibrant hues, unconventional shapes, and geometric patterns.

Describe the colors and designs on your wedding invitations.

What vibe did your wedding invitations send? Fun, elegance?

Who did your invitations list as the wedding hosts? Parents, bride and groom?

Did you pepper the invitations with popular '80s slang? If so, give an example.

How did you send out your wedding invitations?

How did your wedding guests RSVP?

Wedding Guests

How many people did you invite to your wedding?

How many guests attended the ceremony?

Could anyone in town attend your '80s wedding—even if they didn't receive a formal invitation?

Did any guests fly in? If so, who and from where?

Wedding Venue

Inspiration for wedding venues came from television shows and magazines, as social media hadn't yet arrived. Popular '80s wedding venues included tourist destinations, the courthouse, as well as grandparents' backyards.

What served as inspiration for your wedding venue? Some couples collected ideas from '80s movies or popular TV shows.

What color palette did you choose for your wedding venue? Hues from the '80s included electric blue, neon pink, and sunshine yellow.

Where did you hold your wedding?

Was it close enough to home so nearby relatives and friends could attend? Or did guests fly in from all over the country?

How did you create a festive wedding atmosphere? String lights, disco balls, balloon arches?

Florals

Wedding florals added stunning visual aesthetics to '80s wedding venues. Though ephemeral, flowers lived a lifetime in wedding photos and memories.

Describe the florals you chose to decorate your wedding venue.

Were your '80s floral decorations extravagant to match the largesse of the decade?

How much did the floral décor cost?

Or did relatives gift the florals for your '80s wedding?

Did skilled relatives or friends create aspects of the floral décor, such as floral arches?

Bridal Shower

Did your friends or family throw you a bridal shower? If so, where was it held?

Did your bridal shower have a theme? If so, what was it?

Who attended your bridal shower?

What gifts did your guests shower you with?

Bachelorette Party

Bachelorette parties were filled with fun and friendship and celebrated the bride's last days of unrivaled freedom.

Did your friends host a bachelorette party?

If so, who attended?

How did you bond with the girls?

What activities, outings, or entertainment did you and your friends enjoy?

What lasting memories did your '80s bachelorette party create?

Wedding Wardrobe

Wedding Gown

Did you purchase your wedding dress? If so, from where?

How much did your wedding dress cost?

Or did you wear a wedding dress that belonged to a family member? If so, who wore it previously?

What color was your wedding dress? Popular colors of the day included ivory, white, and cream.

What materials did your wedding gown consist of? Rich materials of the era included satin, lace, and silk.

Did your '80s wedding dress consist of a decadent amount of fabric?

Did you handmake any part of your wedding gown? If so, what part?

If your wedding dress featured lace, was it decorated with sequins and beads?

How embellished was the train of your dress?

Describe whether your '80s wedding dress had puffy sleeves, a voluminous skirt, enormous bows, or a supersized veil.

Did you follow tradition and wear "something old, something new, something borrowed, and something blue"? If so, describe how you incorporated these elements.

As you walked down the aisle wrapped in luxury, did it feel like a romantic fairy tale?

Did you wear the wedding dress of your dreams?

Bridal Gloves

Lacy, fingerless gloves were all the rage in the '80s!

Did you wear gloves on your wedding day?

If so, describe them.

Bridal Veil

How voluminous was your veil?

If your wedding veil featured ruffle, did it add desirable height to your look?

Bridal Shoes

What color were your wedding shoes?

Did your '80s wedding shoes feature bows?

Where did you buy your wedding shoes?

Wedding Jewelry

What jewelry pieces did you wear for your '80s wedding?

If you wore a necklace to accentuate your bridal look, describe it.

Did you wear oversized earrings?

Did you wear jewelry handed down from previous generations?
If so, describe the heirloom and to whom it belonged.

Hair and Makeup

Bridal makeup in the '80s was bold, reflecting the era's flamboyance. Think electric blue eyeshadow, heavy blush, and frosted pink lipstick.

Who did your hair and makeup on your wedding day? Family, friends, professionals?

Did you go to the salon to have your hair done before the wedding?

If you hired a stylist, how much did it cost?

Did you opt for the "big hair" and "big makeup" that defined the '80s?

How would you describe your wedding day hairdo? Bouffant, teased bangs?

Did you wear an oversized '80s wedding headband or tiara?

Bridesmaids

Bridesmaid dresses in the '80s came in pastel hues, like baby blue, pink, and light green.

Who were your bridesmaids, and how many did you have?

Did the bridesmaids wear gowns identical in design, color, and pattern or mismatched dresses?

Photographer
or Videographer

Videography surged in the '80s, and brides sought out videographers
to record their special day.

Did you hire a photographer or videographer to capture your '8Os wedding?

How much did you spend on professional wedding photos or videos?

How long did the photoshoot last?

Or did friends take your wedding photos?

Describe your best wedding photo and what made it so memorable.

Flashes from the '80s Wedding Past

Flashes from the '80s Wedding Past

Bridal Bouquet

Bridal bouquets in the '80s consisted of lovely florals, like baby's breath, gardenias, and Lilliputian buds. Wedding bouquets symbolized fresh beginnings, romance, and–true to '80s style–extravagance.

Did you carry a cascading bouquet?

If not, how would you describe your bouquet?

List the flowers layered in your bridal bouquet.

Did you preserve your bouquet after the wedding? If so, do you still have it in some form?

Did you press the wedding flowers, creating a brand-new sentimental item?

If you chose not to preserve your wedding bouquet, do you wish you had?

Bouquet Toss

Did you toss your bouquet? If so, who caught it?

Did the unmarried ladies compete to catch it? Or did guests try to avoid catching it, separating like the Red Sea?

Wedding Superstitions

Did you hold wedding superstitions or follow traditions, like those that follow? How did they influence your special day?

Superstition

Seeing each other prior to the wedding was bad luck.

Superstition

The one who caught the bride's bouquet would marry next.

Tradition

The song choice for the newlywed's first dance set the tone for the marriage.

Tradition

Cutting the cake together symbolized unity in the marriage.

Tradition

Feeding wedding cake to each other demonstrated a commitment to provide for one another.

Describe any other wedding superstitions you believed in or traditions you observed.

Processional

What music played as you made your entrance?

How did you feel walking down the aisle?

Did someone escort you down the aisle? If so, who?

Did flower girls participate in your ceremony?

Who was your ring bearer?

Opening Remarks

Who served as your wedding officiant?

Did the officiant express what marriage meant to you?

Readings or Poems

Did you perform a wedding reading or poem?

If so, what lines or verses did you choose?

Vows

Wedding vows, whether heartfelt or lighthearted, expressed a promise to love and commit to a partner.

Did you write your own vows?

If not, did you opt for traditional vows?

Did you read the vows from a book? Or did you memorize your vows?

What emotions ran through you as you listened to the groom recite his vows?

Ring Exchange

Rings have symbolized marriage for 3,000 years. Couples have come a long way since rings made of reeds.

How did it feel to exchange wedding rings?

Do you recall saying what the ring meant to you?

Unity Ceremony

Couples participated in a unity ceremony, performing an act together to symbolize their union. The ritual of lighting a unity candle soared to popular heights during the '80s.

Did you and your partner participate in a unity ceremony?

If so, what ceremony did you perform together?

Closing Remarks

The wedding officiant may have offered words of encouragement, read a requested poem, or offered a prayer.

Did the officiant say any closing remarks?

If so, what parts of them do you recall?

Recessional

What music played during your recessional?

What emotions welled up inside you as you walked down the aisle newly married?

Wedding Reception

Reception Entrance

How did guests react to your newlywed status?

What song played during your wedding entrance?

Speeches and Toasts

Describe the most memorable lines from the wedding speech or toast.

Who offered these unforgettable words?

Cake

Wedding cakes in the '80s trended large, representing the decade's showy excess. Some cakes teetered four tiers high, while others towered eight tiers over guests.

What was the size of your '80s wedding cake? If it had tiers, list how many.

How was your wedding cake decorated?

Who made your wedding cake? Relatives, a bakery?

What flavors did your wedding cake consist of?

Did you save the top tier of your wedding cake to be eaten on your first anniversary?

Food

While big '80s weddings stood out, small backyard ceremonies with homemade cake, mingling, and fun were equally memorable.

Who prepared the food for your wedding? Friends, relatives, caterer?

If you hired a caterer, how many courses did you serve?

Alternatively, did you budget for simple food, like cake, coffee, and sandwiches?

Entertainment

Music

Newlyweds often requested '80s tunes with infectious pop sounds that put guests in a fun mood.

Song choices included
"Come On Eileen" by Dexys Midnight Runner
"The Safety Dance" by Men Without Hats
"I Melt with You" by Modern English

List the songs played at your wedding.

Did your wedding have a DJ?

Did you hire a live band?

Dances

What song did you first dance to as newlyweds?

What song played during the father-and-bride dance?

What song played during the mother-and-groom dance?

What song played during the mother-and-bride dance?

Games

Games that entertained '80s wedding guests included karaoke, wedding trivia, and dance-offs.

What games did guests play at your wedding?

Gifts

List your three favorite wedding gifts.

_____

_____

_____

Did you receive personalized gifts? If so, describe one.

Did you receive tech gifts highly coveted in the '80s, like a VCR, pocket television, or camcorder?

List three useful wedding gifts you received.

_____

_____

_____

Getaway Car

Top-tier '80s wedding cars included Rolls Royce, Jaguar, and Ferrari, as well as practical vehicles, like Buick, GMC pickup, and Corvette.

Did you and your new spouse hop into a getaway car?

If so, what was the model of the car?

If the getaway car was decorated, describe the ceremonial regalia.

Express how it felt to ride off as a newly married couple.

Honeymoon

Tropical locales, like Hawaii and the Caribbean, were popular '80s
honeymoon destinations.

Where did you spend your honeymoon?

**Did you stay in a hotel? If so, which one? If not, where did
you stay?**

How long was your honeymoon?

Did you enjoy the honeymoon phase? If so, how many weeks, months, or years did it last?

Cost

The price of weddings in the '80s ranged from a few hundred dollars to a few thousand, depending on how lavishly the couple wished to spend. Some couples valued the vows and celebrating with people they loved while others preferred to throw an extravaganza.

How much did you budget for your '80s wedding?

How much did you actually spend on your '80s wedding?

Did you go into debt paying for your wedding?

Did relatives contribute financially to your '80s wedding?

List the breakdown of expenses for your '80s wedding.

Venue: _____

Wedding Dress: _____

Food and Drinks: _____

Entertainment: _____

Was the cost of your wedding worth every penny? Why or why not?

Wedding Intangibles

Do you feel '80s weddings were simpler, easier to plan, and less stressful? If so, explain.

Did you make arrangements via mail or in person back in the '80s, unlike today where bookings are commonly made online?

Do you feel the wedding industry has shifted since the '80s?
Provide an example.

Do you feel guest expectations for wedding ceremonies have
changed in the last forty years? If so, how?

Do you believe a "cake and punch reception" would no longer satisfy wedding guests today? Why or why not?

Do you think today's weddings are "major productions" (overpriced and over-the-top) in comparison to '80s weddings? If so, illustrate with an example.

When planning your '80s wedding, did you feel you had nothing to prove, unlike today?

What meaning did your '80s wedding hold for you?

What was the worst (if any) part of your '80s wedding?

What was the best part of your '80s wedding?

Looking back, did you create the '80s wedding day you envisioned?

More Flashes from the '80s Wedding Past

More Flashes from the '80s Wedding Past

Here's to an Unforgettable '80s Wedding!

By taking a leisurely sojourn back to your '80s wedding via this journal, you record the memorable details that younger generations, from adult children on the brink of marriage to curious youth, are sure to draw inspiration from. Wide-eyed and eager, they'll learn about the drama, glitz, and glamour that went into making an '80s ceremony totally worth experiencing and recollecting.

Now that's bodacious!

Books in the
What Was It Like series

What Was It Like Growing Up in the 80s?
A Journal to Revisit and Share the Totally Awesome 80s

What Was It Like During Christmas in the 80s?
A Journal to Revisit and Share the 80s Holiday Spirit

What Was It Like Growing Up in the 90s?
A Journal to Revisit and Share the Rad 90s

What Was It Like During Christmas in the 90s?
A Journal to Revisit and Share the 90s Holiday Vibe

What Was It Like Marrying in the 80s?
A Journal (for Him) to Revisit and Share 80s Wedding Bliss

What Was It Like Marrying in the 90s?
A Journal (for Her) to Revisit and Share 90s Wedding
Magic

www.ingramcontent.com/pod-product-compliance
Lightning Source LLC
Chambersburg PA
CBHW041041050426

42335CB00056B/3244